◁ I DO NOT THINK
THAT I COULD LOVE
A HUMAN BEING ◁

JOHANNA SKIBSRUD
ᖾ I DO NOT THINK THAT I COULD LOVE A HUMAN BEING ᖾ

GASPEREAU PRESS LIMITED
Printers & Publishers
2010

ACKNOWLEDGEMENTS

Thank you to everyone at Gaspereau Press, especially to
Andrew, for his editorial suggestions, patience, and contin-
ued support. Also, thanks to Stephanie Bolster for her help
with the "Measuring Depth" poems in their early stages,
Jessica Moore for her thoughtful readings, friendship, and
advice and to the Elizabeth Bishop House in Great Village,
Nova Scotia, for providing me with the time and space with-
in which to complete the final draft of this manuscript. "Big
Pock," "After Drinking too Much Gin" and "Or perhaps we
will never enter our lives at all, but remain always some-
what at the door of things?" all appeared previously in *The
Canadian Journal of Poetry and Critical Writing* (Spring 2009).

Measuring Depth

HALFWAY ROCK

Just a mile from the rock,
which Ed points to and says,
I took my parents' boat out there
when I was nine, we sit; our
sails as slack as sleeves.

Imagine.

Getting no nearer, no
farther away.

At the centre of the island,
a tall stone cairn.

Raised, Ed says, *by a German sailor who*
survived more than a week of winter there;
only rescued when a woman, hanging
laundry out to dry saw his
stand of stones from shore.

We unlash the oars to raise them, and when we
stand them up, they're tall.

Until the Coast Guard came to take me home, Ed says,
I didn't know I'd gone too far.

Ben counts. *One, two, three, four. Row!* He yells out,
        Row!

        Remember,

        I write this poem with nearly
        five months retrospect, and so

I know that Ed is dead now, having,
late in August, driven off a steep
embankment from the road, after
nodding briefly off in late sun one afternoon.

We row and row.

Halfway to what? Diana asks.

But Ed says, *Wait,*
and drops his oar.

Is that, he asks, *some wind?*

He shakes his arms, then holds them out,
palms up, head tilted back,
and both eyes closed.
His eyelids and his throat exposed.

Do this, he says.
Communicate with aliens.

But there's not a breath of it to feel.

No wind, says Will. *No wind,* I say.

Row, Ben says. *Row, Ed. Row.*

Which begs the question:
Why write this poem in present tense,
knowing what I know?

Leaning again into his oar, Ed says:
It felt too good out there to turn back home.
It's friggin far, though—

for a nine-year-old, I mean.

Un, deux, trois, quatre!
Ben yells, to keep us moving,
Una, dos, tres, quatro!
He yells again.

For anyone, Diana says.
If there isn't any wind.

> And what determines that a man survives,
> when there's no good reason that he should?

> Saved, finally, by a woman hanging laundry out to dry.

Eins, Zwie, Drei, Vier.

> Or that a man dies, when there's
> no reason on this earth he should.

You count like a German, Ben, Ed yells,
but you sure as hell don't row like one.

> Well there isn't, is there?

> No reason on this earth, at all.

Row! Ed yells, again.

Throwing, with the word, his weight,
heavily to oar.

MAST

Uprooted, it's a heavy, awkward thing.

Ed and I, at bow-watch, look for rocks,
and shallow ground.

An osprey wings by.

A seal, curious,
follows at some distance.

Under the bridge it's
cool and dark, and when we yell—
just one long note—we hear it
resonate, rib to rib, inside.

Once more in open air,
Ed and I do a dance up on the rail,
and lean into the wire.

Then he bends, picks
seaweed from the hull,
and turns,

wears it like a moustache; his
lip squeezed to his nose.

I'll pay you Tuesday, for a hamburger today,
he says, bowing. Extending,

generally, a hand.

IN LIGHT OF THIS, AS I'VE
LIVED ON BOARD THIS BOAT

It was, then, the way I like it best:
made, as I was, by weather, so aware.
By the contrast of the sun and cold,
each so separate on my skin.

It's nearly always like that.
In the excess or the absence of a thing that I
appreciate it best. The way I wish I always
could. By plunging myself deeply into it, I mean,
and taking up, within it, all the space I can.

Looking back, it's just, there always seems to be more
room within each moment than, originally, I'd thought.
So that it's only, then, in retrospect, that I
explore each moment, truly; only *then* take that great pleasure,
and that's so sad.

That I *do that*—and, I do.
Imagine my moments, as I first possess them,
to be so small that I just splash right through,
and don't notice at first, or particularly,
the space available to me there,
which only later I realize I can fill.

In light of this, I want always to
live as I have lived on board this boat.
To be, always, like this: tired when I sleep,
hungry when I sit to eat, and when I love I want to love
as recklessly as this: when I've been,
in my loneliness, desiring.

I want to recollect my moments in their wholeness,
without neglecting to possess them, truly, first.
Without neglecting to stretch myself, like this, fully into them,
each one, as I would stretch out on a deck to air.
Resting, in the absence of any wind. Protected,
in a harbour there, and neither hot nor cold, but rather
both at once; the contrast, for a moment, so
apparent on my skin.

MEASURING DEPTH: LEAD LINE IN FOG

On another day I might remember it as rain.

The fog, as it was,
so thick and wet we hardly see him:

Ed, at bow. His yell quite

      separate from his body—
      and that too—

          faint

(*Ten feet,* he's yelled to stern, having
turned there from the bow).

Yes, the fog so thick—so dense, and still, and cold—
that on another day I might remember only:

      I was wet: that it was rain.

It makes the distance, just
      him to us, appear
        much larger,
as though it is a single motion
that he makes up there, at bow.

      The cast. The turn. And then the
      glance to where the rope is pinched.

      The yell stopped short by fog.
      A measurement, to stern.

Stopped short by fog so wet, so thick,
        so nearly rain

        that we
        (first me, then she—Diana)
        must pass the words,
        ten feet, along the deck
        'til Tom, who's at the tiller, finally hears.

Just *that:* ten feet.

Even with this distance that we've traveled now from shore.

Measured out, and measured out again—no deeper—until we grow
accustomed to that depth,

        that sound,

                those words.

                Which we pass along to stern. Each of us so

isolate, and so resigned, that we find ourselves
        surprised when Ed yells out

                fifteen!

His fingers further on the line.

It seems (even after all that
time spent waiting) quite sudden now.

And someone:

You sure there, Ed? We still got
                bottom?

(Quite certainly it's fog,
I should make that point quite clearly.

Remember that—remember *this*—
in just this way—

this present moment, as if it were already in the past,
so that later I can retrieve it just 'as it was' just
as it is).

Which is a fog.

(Again, the plunge.)

Not rain.

Yep, Ed says. *Still got fifteen*, and Tom, he hears this time,
without my help,
without Diana.

(This means,
what? The fog has thinned?)

A bit of silence, now—
or, no—

It's just the lead I hear, which bumps along the bow.

Just that, and nothing more until
another sudden yell

rings out.

Even in this densest fog (which, must surely now, it seems, be thinning) we hear his yell, quite plain:

No bottom! Ed has said.

(I make a point of that, so I'll remember ...

the way his voice has sounded now ...

has sounded, then.

So exuberant in declaration ... then ...)

And we're clear of ground, and into water
which is now immeasurable.

To us, I mean;
        this length of line.

Arriving at Giza through the Back Fence

YOU SPENT ALL DAY AT THE WATER

You spent all day down at the water,
in and out with your mask and your
waterproof shoes. To me, you were just
the round of your back at your shoulders
floating slowly in circles.

We could not have been more
distant, then, and from above it might have been
easy to imagine, as we were not yet
able to do, that we were

made to live that away,
apart from one another: me on land,
and you in water, just your
raised back visible to me,
in circles, until the sun went down somewhere.

Once, though, when I swam out
and saw your face, distorted
by the water and the mask, I thought:
this is the closest that we've ever been.

We couldn't speak, or touch each other.
We were like babies, a little unborn,
and everything was new, then,
and unspeaking, and clumsy, but we had
an incredible wonder, an incredible
acceptance of things.

Then, behind you, I saw a thousand small lights where
a school of fish had gathered, surrounding you entirely.
It was a great glow. The most beautiful
thing, I think, that I have ever seen.

Then you turned and saw them, too. I saw your
face change behind your mask, and we remained
like that. Unspeaking, not touching. Witnesses
together of that strange and most
beautiful thing.

So, I understand it. Why you came back
pale and not quite yourself each time from the beach.
It is so intricate, all of it; there are so many parts,
and each one is so separate and so
often beautiful that it is startling
to find it out again, and then over again—how
even our limited planet, our own small, known, globe,
exceeds the very edge of vastness sometimes,
and of comprehension.

Ordinarily, we reserve that wonder for stars and planets and
other celestial things, but the ocean's just the same, and
plunging your head below the surface
you were as distant, then, and as overwhelmed
as though you'd plunged your head among the stars,
and seen the way the universe was
specific and measureless and unconstrained,
where we'd been thinking all this time,
from our relative distance, that it was
perceivable and vague.

Still, it was you more than I that was affected.
Perhaps because I had, on another occasion,
been underwater. At the age of thirteen,
on a Caribbean vacation. Or that I'd
spent more time in and out of it, having
grown up by the ocean.

I had all along, imagined it, and from
an early age so that—although still

inscrutable and vast—it became for me an
agreeable incomprehension, which
I accepted; like heaven.

CLIMBING THE MINARET AT
BARQUQ ONE AFTERNOON

Reaching, at last, the highest point,
from which we can go no further,
we find, to our surprise, that
everything is simple;
laid before us.
All that we have ever
seen, or dreamed of,
or imagined.
Reduced suddenly,
to lineation,
to hints of
essences, like
poems.

WHEN I AM CALLED TO STAND

O my heart, do not stand as a witness against me in the tribunal.
SPELL 30, THE EGYPTIAN BOOK OF THE DEAD

When I am called to stand
and give account of things,
heart, do not tell the whole story.

Do not stutter, pause, divulge, or
admit that if I could I would remain.

That, in truth, I was not expecting to be called.

That I had thought—having
gone so long now, and so alone—
I could escape this too.

That we could
                    remain; could
live alone and unexamined
within these walls—this

            false body—
            and not be called
            in order to

betray each other in the end.

Heart, do not stand as witness against me in the tribunal.
Let some of all of this be lost.

Let it be sealed. Let it be cauterized in chasms,
in each of your four chambers. But

do not preserve it there. Let it
      rot. Let it

stink and burst in the
retracted annals of the body. Let it
dissolve itself in

liquid and in gas; let it not ask questions that it
cannot answer, but neither let it be

borne aloft by incantation, invocation, or appeal.

O heart, resist. And if you
cannot, let us

make a pact. Let's seal it. Let us not
answer for this,
or for our
      selves. Let us
      not stand trial. Let us
      slip away now, heart; let's
         go.

I pulled the head of my horse up to stop at the gate, while
Mahmoud helped the sentinel take down a section of fence
and let us pass.

By then, the sun was setting. Discretely, to the left. And
from its central point, the city spread in two directions.

We drank a Coca-Cola and surveyed the land.

It was as though it was the city, then, and its inhabitants,
which were the very limit of imagination.

PRAYER FOR NINA ELLEN DURING SANDSTORM

Around four o'clock the wind picked up and a small sandstorm obscured most of the valley. We had climbed, by then, onto the high part of the hill where the ruins were less vibrant than the ones below, consisting mostly of the rounded mouths of empty passageways, and hollowed stone.

We stood for several minutes and watched as the white squall billowed its way in great plumes from the valley, in the direction that we'd come. Then we descended. Quickly; the sand stinging at our faces, to the lower road by which we could continue on to the small village we had seen for some time from a distance: its lone minaret.

ONE AFTERNOON, PAUSED IN FRONT OF
PAUL KLEE'S THE MAGIC GARDEN

Not that I would be a child again, exactly, and build my small cities with
sticks and mud in the mossy patches of the track which ran through the
back woods of my parents' place where no one would find them (that, an
enterprise that would take whole afternoons, and the result of which—

always both disastrous and sublime—I discovered one day reproduced
flawlessly in Paul Klee's *The Magic Garden* while floating through the
vertical white halls of that museum. We interrupted our slow travel
only once: to step outside where the crowds gathered, and laugh out
loud at Marino Marini's horse and rider, which hailed the city with his
immutable erection), but that I would be somehow that *instance,*
however fleeting, in which I find myself

again sometimes to be the cities—long unbuilt or crumbling—of my
childhood. To be at once, like that: sticks, paper. But also: fathomless,
unknown. Just as my backyard had always, in those days, two selves,
which were constantly in doubt of one another; I mean, of both the
earthbound and the transcendent kingdoms.

BRUNO HELPS HIMSELF TO TOMATOES

Not long ago, I read a poem that Bruno wrote,
about tomatoes, and other fruit.

One after the other the foods were named.

Halfway through I was hungry and didn't
notice when, in the last few lines the mood
shifted, and he mentioned love.

What is it, I wonder, that he is thinking now?

As he stirs together the oil and the vinegar,
which will soon

spill over the vegetables, and the

wet seeds of the tomatoes,
which now lie exposed on his plate?

Is he thinking about love? Or, is he
imagining, as I imagine,

the tomatoes, when he
first bites into them:

how they will draw the spit
from underneath his tongue,
and the corners of his mouth?

Getting Dressed in the Usual Way

᷉

BIG POCK

Always the same time of year I get to feeling lonely for it.
How I stood above Big Pock and would not run it, and how I would
run it now. How I would, now, shoulder my boat and lay it down,
without a thought, in that blind eddy and strike out. My bow
pointed, at first, upstream, until spinning and charging through
cross waves, it carries me all the way down, my
heart in my throat like a fish to the flat water below.

How, for plain joy, I would roll my boat down there
until my head spins. And the mountains, and water, and trees,
how they would be kaleidoscope; I, the small glass turning,
they, the steady wheel.

I can not help it, though, sometimes, to wonder—*would I?*
Run that river were I set there now? In body. In fact.
And not just in mind, wandering back; to that more
specious afternoon, made airy and idle by time?

Would I, with my boat over my shoulder and both feet
cold in run-off water, in this—this *actual* moment—
run? Or is it, more likely, only from this presumptuous,
invulnerable range that I can say I had it in me then,
and would again?

Is this, then, the best of things? Just: the idea of it.
The trees, the river, solid, and me, spinning. How I must have
felt that way sometime, and do again, in odd moments.
My joy, allowed a turn, being
great inside.

MACKENZIE RIVER DELTA: FIRST THAW

I love the flowers that you tell me about on my twenty-seventh birthday
saying, this year you'll have to use your imagination. How they
stand; each separate, and yet still integral to one another,
flawless; with the eucalyptus, in their vase.

Just as we, from our different vantage points—you at
your end of the world and I at another—also stand. Having
achieved perfection at twenty-seven, just like we
said we would.

Having projected ourselves out, that is, along those
same lines—that
longhand of desire—which,
        though shapely, is still, of course,

inarticulate somehow. Yes, shapely. Nearly
statuesque some mornings (when, as onto that
blank page, first waking, we have yet to retire from
the illimitable possibility of dreaming into
the available rhetoric of day)—and yet

mute, unspeaking, having only the rudimentary vocabulary,
after all, of human beings. And, now—worse,
in absence, our voices, detached, are left only wandering, on uncertain
telephone lines, above the vast Canadian shield, over

Nunavutian tundra, and across the great Arctic expanses of
permafrost and juniper, where, in this
mid-season, there are no flowers arriving either by
boat or by plane. And yet, through that

transmigration, somehow, all of this—desire—is not
dispersed, dispelled, but instead a more
essential route across that distance is lain, as though it
really was not a vague or an arbitrary course, but that a
single line extended from one end to the other, as a
         string of words along a page.

No, not my poetry—but yours. In its
precision; its brief sentences; its nine syllables to the line.

A desire, which—though in part for one another—is,
at the same time, for something else, as well—ungraspable—
that will perhaps never be satisfied, in truth, in any
long anticipated reunion:

is, again, a longing only for that

vague, illusive thing that sent us into fits of
love, and of despair, as children—when we were

comfortless creatures, and wanting, still, some
         abstract resolution to things. For roses in the
ideal, and not for those that,
if realized, would no doubt be already

wilted, tipped with brown; disguised by
baby's breath, and cellophane.

But—that we conceive, at least, of the
conclusion of this desire in one another is, at times, nearly

good enough, and is why I love imaginary flowers
best; when, on my twenty-seventh birthday,
you give them to me, with their eucalyptus, in their vase.

It would be a sad life, though, to
sustain myself this way, only abstract
rose to rose, and, next year would settle for some
    less than perfect offering. For
the common carnation, for example:
predictable, and edged with brown;
    for the prosaic

crinkle of packaging; for the proximity of
imperfect limbs, cold feet, and untidy rooms; for the occasion of

fatigue, of unwashed teeth, of
    indeterminate sadnesses.

Although, having once sent ourselves, our
inarticulate love, out—broadcast it over the great
arch of wilderness that separates the poles—
we cannot return by old lines, cannot
resign ourselves.

AFTER DRINKING TOO MUCH GIN

When, after having shown you to the door, I sat
down at the table again, I kept going
almost to the floor.

Funny the way everything seems to run in.

For example, it did not feel like it was
the floor that I was headed toward—

      no.

It was the floor by
         accident, by
intervention, and as though
         otherwise
I might have existed in entirely
         different terms.

In illimitable landscapes,
ever-broadening horizons—

and not just in terms,
like this, of up or down.

The melt-off water, in a single vein, has
split the long drive,
and outside, and all around, there is a great
rushing sound.

OR PERHAPS WE WILL NEVER ENTER
OUR LIVES AT ALL, BUT REMAIN ALWAYS
SOMEWHAT AT THE DOOR OF THINGS?

Repeat ourselves, in the cramped and inner
chambers of our hearts, where, in ever-narrowing circles, we

rotate the room, only to wake up with the same
headache as last year, having been

stuffed, and to the same degree, by
food and wine;

having made the same
derisive comments about
making a living; having

recommended the same book, and championed
equally the allure of
hotpot cooking and Sophie Calle; having

laughed at the same—millisecond too soon—point in a story that
in all honesty I've yet to hear; having

stared always, and too long, at the same
clock on the wall, the same

photograph above the same narrator's head, without
identifying a single object.

Having returned, unstumbling,
disastrously cool, to seemingly

uninhabited rooms and ingested, over the spiraling
drain of the stained sink, quantities of lukewarm water,

and having stared, into the open jaw of the fridge
to the same contents there, and having

without satisfaction eaten the same sandwich, and slipped
into the same rotarian sleep: as though
head and legs swung,

back and forth, by oblique angles, toward
the same, undiscoverable
end.

GETTING DRESSED IN THE USUAL WAY ON THE DAY
YOU TOLD ME YOU DIDN'T LOVE ME ANYMORE

This morning, the false pearls that we
bought, at the little shop off the Place D'Odeon
which we stumbled on—twice—last fall,

after having wandered there from the university
and eaten crepes, knee to knee, in the Rue Mouffetarde,

leaving Iqbal to steer your parents home through the
Luxembourg gardens.

They had seemed to me, then, a treasure of such
rare beauty, that I could not a second time pass them by,
and you did not refuse me.

Then, the bracelet that you found, and brought to me
from Marrakech, which, this morning, I

place on my wrist in the usual way, with the utmost

attention and care, just as
once, and for the first time, you

placed it there for me, in a
pink Milanese hotel room after what had
seemed such a

long time. Who knew that we would
afterwards spend so many
nights apart; a whole lifetime.

Or in pink. That

absurd and splendid bed, the luxury of our
Chungbuk days, in whose weekends I had

absorbed myself entirely—as though they
contained in their

hours the formula for all my future happinesses, which I
could, on those occasions, name.

And the small circles on the
white shells of the earrings that you
chose for me in a Bangkok market, and that I
wore, all through Asia, and
in Egypt matched perfectly the scarf that you

undid for me sometimes at the end of the day.

Their spirals beginning and
ending, repeatedly, like waves—a
little of the beach that we
took with us from our brief
sojourn there. Where we discovered an entire,
crystalline, underworld all our own. The fishes in
bursts, in spasms. And where we
reclined later, in the first bloom of our new health after an

inexplicable rainy-season flu, in which
for seven days we were

suspended parallel, in the jungle, the
ceiling fan stirring the thick air like a spoon. How
desperately we wanted to
comfort one another, then; to lift the
painful thing which crouched like a cat in our
brains. To get

rid of it entirely; to throw it out, and live
together in quiet rooms where we would
take always great
care with one another, and we
would not die.

This morning, in the usual way, I have
lifted them, one by one, from their
wooden box, which I carried home from China.

These proofs, however fleeting, of my
great and terrifying expectations, and
boundless love.

I will retrieve them only briefly now.

From where, buried in their painted landscape,
they will be kept, original and whole.

Guarded by thin cows, and mountains;
by courtly, one-dimensioned men, and the four corners
of a circumscribed, right-angled sky.

A single and impenetrable plane—
a Chinese landscape; that

unfathomable countryside, which was also the
ultimate and unfamiliar region I imagined I was looking for
when, with unmitigated patience,
and unswerving devotion, I

dug and dug as a child, out back in the yard.

IMAGE OF A MAN STEPPING
FROM A CURB INTO OPEN AIR

Strange vertigo when you think of it. An always nearly
        dropping away.

Picture it. Like this:

           The leading foot eternally
                  thrust and hovering.

I AM MISS RUMPHIUS THIS MORNING

I am Miss Rumphius this morning.

The turning point, where,
in her city clothes, she visits the conservatory,
dreaming of tropical islands; of Africa.

I float through the orchids
and memorize their names.

Brother Elizabeth;
brother Janet.

Linger sometimes, under
the sheltering spoon of a leaf, and think
of the small mice of the storybooks
who set off on journeys
in just this way, with only

the clothes on their back; who
sought shelter at night under
broad-backed leaves, like these.

It's true. There is such a fortune to be had,
for those who will have it; no,
it is not in

false pursuit that mice go
lumbering off, out of doors.
We assure children as much, we make
great promises.

If, years later, backed into a corner we say:
It is neither true nor untrue,
that is the concession we make.

There are certain
things, we will say, for which you will—
quite simply—not be prepared.

The blue taro, for example, will
catch you off guard. The evening prince,
the Georges Seurat. Even the slumberous
elephant ear, which grows prosaically

thick-skinned, and close to the ground.

I cannot be certain of anything this morning. I am
Miss Rumphius: absurdly, extravagantly alone,
a quarter through the book, just
                    setting out.

I wonder. Did she, like me, also pause on certain days over the
South African succulents—and marvel at them; the way they
grow, always full, and wet, and round,

and do not, in the continued
inarticulation of a deep and indescribable craving,
explode from an impatience that wells from the root?

Did she speculate sometimes if it would be
best to grow—like the American

elm or willow—large and wild? Bending, for example,
over the steep embankments of the highways along which she

walked from the garden to town, some
whistling thought in her head.

Or if it would be preferable, like in the Eastern Garden, to
grow as the Chinese sweet plum, aged 70 years: in eloquent
curves and spirals. To exist

neatly, as a symbol of itself—instead of,
like the scrubby spruce, the elm, endlessly

exaggerating things with
gangly, overgrown, protrusive limbs; each year
blatant, and unaccountable, in loops and rings.

A quarter through; some
uncertainty now after years of
childish desiring. Of the
necessary, initial, over-simplification of things.

Thinking, this is not it yet.

"Tossed on membraneous wings,"
Miss Rumphius, and me, somewhat
winged this morning, in the middle of the book. No,
certain of nothing now, I would be a

Chinese sweet plum and a great
elephant ear at once, I would
find a middle course, sink

deeply into an infinity of
spirals, grow

rings and rings.

Still a Voyage

Visiting the places of early childhood years later when you are dying is a different sort of sadness than I'd thought that it would be. In the park, the rink is lit, though it is empty. Did I expect

a man and his small child to skate in circles forever there?

Not surprising, the park is not as large as I had thought, or far; now the distances between things have begun to go. Off Albert, onto Nelson, I walk along and look at the houses in rows. First, the grey house, the brick house, the cat house, then the wide red townhouse that you lived in for a while. It is not

terrifying as I had once believed it to be. There are no men sitting out on the porch tonight to call me 'boy', as there once had been. Things get easier to bear. Still, I am like a kite tonight trailing after me my long tail.

When I arrive—past the tall house and Miss Amey's—I stand for a long time, looking in from the street. No—nothing is taken away. It is all still here, underneath, it must be. Things do not just disappear, you know.

I have told myself it will be smaller than I have remembered it to be, and it is. I think I could pick the whole place up, and swallow it, and carry it around with me, inside. And now that you are dying and there is nothing left to say, I could take it to you. I could open up my chest, and you would see it, glowing there. I could say, see?

I remember everything.

And the tall tree, in the backyard, the black walnut, the one thing that has not diminished in size, would push its long branches through my arms and fingers, and shoot its roots out past my toes. It would rise up, behind me, when I am too weak or irresolute to stand: immutable, and tall.

In adulthood, I have found that it is just the spaces between things that go and that other than that everything is the same. We are not so damaged by things as we once had supposed. No, there is nothing to be sorry for, now. Look, I was a happy child.

Now I will walk all the way to Princess Street; past the old house, the tree, and the yard. Goodbye to you—pink house, small house, grey house, blue house. No, it is not

sadness, it is something different now. Things get easier to bear. It is as though I were climbing into my own life inside out, like a glove. As though I were a very thin kite, all alone in a strange land, trailing after me a long tail, which gets

tied to things, and pulls, and pulls. Small things. A sudden memory—arisen from somewhere. Red shoes, I remember. Crackerjacks, a certain

honey-coloured rabbit I recall. I would follow that line, trace it back. I would gather everything that we have scattered here, inside, and say to you, when it is time: look, look in; I've kept everything.

Say, all is as it was, and will be: there is nothing to be sorry for, regret, or leave behind. I have gathered it up, made a soft place inside,

we're safe.

WALKING ONE NIGHT IN AN UNFAMILIAR TOWN, IT SNOWS

What is it in me that, like an inverted telescope, makes me see things always the wrong way round?

So that it is the universe that seems from here to be so small and far away. Me that's solid. Immutable and vast.

When, in truth, already I begin to dim. Already I am nearly burned away. While outside everything still spins and lengthens, as along
                electrical wire.

Yes. Comparatively burned away, though inside I seem to smolder on; I believe I'll last another hundred-billion years.

But it begins. It positively presses in. You start to feel it. Things happens to you: then, and then, and no longer in the way, both simultaneous and rare, of stars, or lights or of the hard and limbless snow.

My thoughts move slowly now, and leave thin tails. Perhaps they've been already thought—a thousand years ago or more?

That their presence in my brain is just, now, the faintest trailing light …?

Already nearly burned away; my forests razed, my animals already dead inside their holes. And yet, still it seems somehow I smolder on; still thoughts dash themselves, a last hoorah, against my brain; dissolve. I have been driven to the core, the burning centre. Am my own last heart beating. *Thrum, thrum, thrum.*

    While all around, the snow too cold to drift.

      Silence.

STILL A VOYAGE

It was not gentle, no. In the end,
it was an accident.

Abhorrent and unforeseen.

A shift somehow: the wind blew
sideways through, there was not
even any sound.

And you—?

A pipe,
an empty-limbed bird.

While all around you
everything grows heavy now.
                    The bird empty,
the bones still open, flown.

No—it was not *gentle*. It was,
instead, original and whole.

A rough birth, a tear, a
fissure of the shell.

And then,

my bird ... my little bird ...

                    lifting?

Broadcast out now, across a
suddenly attainable landscape?

I would not let it in, or let you out, whatever
language you would have me use.

It is, to be alive, to be to a certain extent

unemptiable. I would make for you a nest of
newsprint by the stove, I would

keep you, and keep you. I would

take you to my lips,

and blow—so that

the wind, again, would
whistle through you;

your lungs inflate
like red balloons.

I would follow you.

High across the yard. Past the bridge,
the fence, the river.

Over dense New Brunswick
forest, past mud flats and marshland;

along the sheltered
Northumberland inlets of my childhood,
which you were not witness to—

Float with you inland, then.

Along the rough and open roads,
of Maine and of Ontario.

Through the dark
and closely-treed channels
of Michigan and Minnesota; as far
South as the Badlands, where we

never now will go,

until—finally—
drifting North, I would
hover with you

above the right-angled farmland of
South and North Dakota; floating

low over the shorn pastures there;

the sunflower fields, the Canadian
geese in droves, the gated
buffalo.

To Fargo. To the one tree there;

alone, you said, in a limitless landscape.

Sit up with you, caught,
on the

high branches.

SCENE FROM WINDOW; NORTH BAY, ONTARIO

Are we, then, the holes in the universe where
everything that we are not, is not?

Cut cleanly, as though from paper, from cloth?

A different world than the one I had imagined:
the opposite of the shadow-puppetry I
practised as a child, and at which I
excelled; creating long dramas late at night in my
bedroom for no one. As there was no one—

not even I who remained
necessarily behind the curtain—

to witness the effect.

AT A CERTAIN POINT,
EVERYTHING BEGINS AGAIN

In the same way that, my eyes crammed shut, I tried, when young, to arrive somehow at the word "infinity," only to reach again that certain and familiar precipice, the small tower I had, myself, constructed of my mind, from where began again only the static buzz of broken or as yet unstrung electrical wire and from where I would lose all signal, so a poem, at a certain distance from itself, will bite its tail; will turn a corner, such as this one, which has just now been turned inside this poem; and though I returned, always defeated— having ascended only my own small tower, no further, having arrived at nothing there—though I have not yet grasped, nor now anticipate grasping hold of anything in the way that I had once imagined, as though to an electric wire, it is, I think, the turn itself that's certain and will last: that furthest extension of the self where the line of thought is at once pulled taut and left to buzz at the end of its wire; see the poem now at its last breath, the final word pushed out on an emptied lung; the brief inhale

IF IN A THOUSAND YEARS

If in a thousand years this
sadness that I am carrying around
with me inside will be burned up;

will fall down and spit like dust to
unknown planets, in particles of
dirt and stone, I can

live with that.

I can let it go. Everything I
have not and
will not do.

I have—my darling—

only sped you on your way.
There is nothing here to

look forward to, or understand.

It is, for you, as though
everything had already
happened, now. As though
you were a planet. The last

remote and quivering matter of a

burned down love.
As though everything
from that long distance,
had already

fallen and fallen;
the stars put out. Already

clanging around in your
head like

spoons in a jar.

Everything Remains to be Spoken of

THIS

This time,
for a while at least, let it
remain

      this.

Illiterate buzz, as of
insects, or bees.

A communicable
absence, somehow—

of thought, certainly,
perhaps even of sound—just,

      this.

Right *here,* right *now,*
this, the

      I, I, I,
      this

thinking or
unthinking thing—
this voice, this hum, this
inarticulate gesticulation
of the heart or mind, this:

opening where there was no
opening before.

This, a
cord, which, pulled, must be
directly fastened to the heart.
This *I!* And this

    you.

Who take from me now these
few and simple things that I own.

A T-shirt. Two shoes.
Easy, like that. We do not

need these things; nor

windows, nor
roofs, there is just—

air out there.

Let's just
keep it like

this. Let's just have

this for a while; a small
fire in us, keep

the animals at bay.

Do not speak to me now

too softly, or at all, I would
hardly have you breathe.

Let alone, like
            this,

begin to beat your heart too
loudly,

explode and—

                    What final darkness will descend?
                    What creeping hunger? What spaces

                    edge themselves between the
                    shapes of gasses and the stars? What vast

                    emptiness will at last reveal itself to be the
                    heart of things?

ON A BAD NIGHT WISHING
TO TURN INTO A BIRD

Not animal but air, which
tangled once and

held shape a moment in your
hand. Which

dreamed itself
bone, which
purported itself

once

to fly. Which

looked out from
dark eyes, all

sense, all
sound, and said:

I will build my
small nest here,
and watch for foxes
all day long,

and feed long
flutes of necks with
food that I will
find, and carry.

COME, POSTMAN

Come, postman, come
climb me.
Come and tell me things.

Come. Whisper low, whisper all
out of breath, I will grow a shady
tree for you up here.

Come. What
news do you bring? What
words, all printed in rows?

Come, postman.
Climb me. Come and
tell me things.

WHAT TOUGHNESS IS IT

What toughness is it in each moment as it comes, that
grows and stretches that which was to bursting,
and becomes what it was not?

Is (must) each instance be like that?

Necessarily more solid, more
thick-skinned than the last?

Is this how time turns me, how I
         evolve; must I

                  become

                  this?

How did 'love', that is, the way we spoke it, turn
red like that, all tooth and claw?

There must be some
softness somewhere. I have not been,
nor will be, made

more durable by time, but
less and less so. Am not even
properly a woman yet. How would I
         become one?

I WAS THINKING OF YOUR FATHER
WHEN NORTH DAKOTA WENT RED

He said, and I, with the phone to my ear,
watch the great map of America, with its
burning centre, turn blue.

The way he would
sit out on his add-on porch with the radio,
as though he were
the last man alive in America.

Of the great sermons that he sent
whistling down 12th East in one or two
monosyllabic notes.

AT THE PARTY

These
rough tools,

hands, eyes,
ears, how

best
to use them?

How best to daily

rough up
the

earth with them? How

raise anything from it?

IN WHICH I IMAGINE MYSELF
CONTAINED WITHIN THE
PAGES OF A BOOK

Where will I
go when I go?

Will I, like

the words of a book
when it's closed
just one day
seem to

disappear?

Think of it.

All closed up, and with no
light getting in;

it will not be
words and darkness,
will it? No. It will be just

darkness then.

But it is not, no,
must not be—so
simple as that;

not just

the body, the mind
which is the being alive,

but the spaces between.

See how it comes?

How, even now, I

fall, am
fallen, like this,
         open—

as though ruffled by something; a thumb
         or a breeze?

Even when
whole days go
by sometimes
when I do not
stir inside myself
and no one comes.

Always, like this—
like a corner, or a door,

whether ventured
into or from—

remaining that way.
A corner. A door.

No, there is no

end, is there. No final
shutting up of things.
It is only the

eye, the mind, for example,
that thinks it may have
travelled in a

straight line through me.
But there is
no straight line, there is
no through me.

It is all, instead,

the roundnesses and
darknesses of things;
the still
un-readness; an

imminent

rustling.

ON HEARING OF THE DEATH OF ROBERT STRANGE MCNAMARA

The steady whine, this morning, of the
neighbour's saw,

and, once, the rise of
a single voice behind the wall.

The cat noses out between
balcony rails, withdraws.

Everything has held.

Only the tomato plant adrift. Only
the mind like a child
wandering.

LAMENT

How sad that the light when I shut my eyes should linger in such precise formation in my mind without having properly illuminated anything.

I DO NOT THINK THAT I COULD LOVE
A HUMAN BEING

I do not think that I could love a human being; I would not
know it if I squeezed too hard. I would be a great bear. I would
go rumbling through.

I would try to eat you. I would stand alone,
in the quiet centre of you, and roar. No, I
could not love you. I could not
love a human being.

I would get so
stuck on things. The small

flaws in you, like

the way that you will die;
it would stick in my throat, I could not love you.

And the way that, if you touched me, I would be
as if to you a solid object,
as if a boot, a stick, a stone.

And you to me. The way that I could

pick you up. That I could
hammer you against me; that I could
bruise myself on you, and still have only a

brief impression of you left there on my skin.

And, if I cried, that too would be
an imitation of the thing that I would feel.

And the pain itself, if it were real, would come as if
so separately from you that it might

equally have been a whip, a rope,
a rail with which I thrashed myself when I

thrashed myself with you.

No, I could not love a human being if they
could not leave a mark.

Even if I were a bear
and I ate you, you would
move right through me.

Even if you were a bear
and you ate me, I would
move right through you.

But I am not a bear. And will not eat you.
If I said I could, I could not.

And you are not a bear. And will not eat me.

And that is why I could not love you.
And that is why I could not love you.
And that is why I could not love you.

EVERYTHING REMAINS TO BE SPOKEN OF

Believe that even in my deliberateness I was not deliberate.
GWENDOLYN BROOKS

I remember once I suggested we might
creep, like foxes, forever forward toward
one another. In order to sit,

at long last, silently, and paw to paw,
at the very limit.

That intimacy was only a matter, then, of

having not noticed the degree, or
method by which it was earned …

And that, having for so long left
everything unsaid—having
still not learned
the names of things—

the possibility now remained.

But, as it was. There was no
space for anything. There was only this,

the space of:

impossible to speak, to swallow.

A space known, except once
by an unlucky stranger,
to no one.

Stranger who, after
six weeks, was scraped out without warning,
and during whose
funereal mumblings we two,
facing one another as though for
the first time

(the first rustlings, then, of form—of
        delineation—)

began to speak; saying,

that is me. And that is you.
And that
        was.

        Was.

Along with other indecipherable syllables;
we had not yet acquired language.

Better, though, now, I think
to burst. To become a sudden swift
loosening of capillaries; an intensification of
thrombic pressure from some
sub-corporeal root.

        But that's just
        it, though. The trick of it.

The way a body can fool you, sometimes, in its
brief, small deaths, so that you come to believe that
the rest will follow.

But it does not. No,
nothing has followed. And I

remain, like this. Untipped,
unspilled; you see how

rapidly I disappear from you now.

Better I think now to be
pumped through with sudden brightness,
to hear the incessant chatter of water,
of air, as it

enters the blood, in order, in all
earnestness, to irrigate the tender
muscle of the heart, where everything
remains, latent and murmuring, under the skin.

As in the time before I knew you;
when I did not speak, or even breathe—when I
climbed high mountains, and sat alone, at the barest,
furthest peak that I could find, and there were

great mysteries; and I
knew them; and, with certainty, that they would roll one day
as if like spools from my tongue.

Typeset in Rod McDonald's Cartier Book by Andrew Steeves
& printed & bound at Gaspereau Press under the direction of
Gary Dunfield.

9   8   7   6   5   4   3   2   1

Library & Archives Canada Cataloguing in Publication

Skibsrud, Johanna Shively, 1980–
I do not think that I could love a human being / Johanna
Skibsrud.

Poems.
ISBN 978-1-55447-085-3

I. Title.

PS8587.K46146 2010   C811'.54   C2010-901221-6

GASPEREAU PRESS LIMITED
Gary Dunfield & Andrew Steeves ❡ Printers & Publishers
47 Church Avenue, Kentville, NS, Canada B4N 2M7
www.gaspereau.com